MW00565981

Quequechan: Forgotten River

Written by Jeanne L. Prevost
Illustrated by Linda Crockett

Quequechan: Forgotten River

by
Jeanne L. Prevost
Illustrated by Linda Crockett

Text copyright © 2008 Jeanne L. Prevost
Illustrations copyright © 2008 Operation Outreach-USA, Inc.

Published by
Operation Outreach-USA Press
Holliston, MA

ISBN 978-0-9792144-2-4

Printed in the United States of America

This book is dedicated to Michelle S. Prevost,
my daughter,
my friend and confidante,
my fellow admirer of woodland beauty,
my hiking and backpacking buddy,
and my most helpful consultant and source of encouragement
in this attempt to describe my deep and abiding appreciation
for the Quequechan River.

-JP

Very, very old was I when the first people
came to me. For thousands of years, I had
lived here embracing fish, birds, plants,
insects, reptiles, amphibians, and
mammals in my wide, watery arms.

Spread out below the clouds, I was an open
invitation to the eagle for fishing, to the deer
for drinking, to the countless other
animals that depended on me.

What's more,
I was beautiful.

During one sunlight long ago, I heard strange
new noises--sounds unlike any ever uttered
along my banks.
Shouts of "Nippe! Wawpatucke! Hammos!"
passed through the spring air.

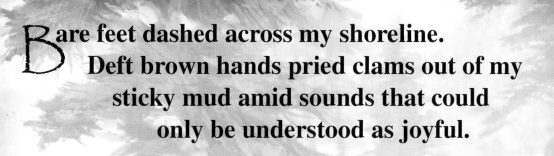

Bare feet dashed across my shoreline.
Deft brown hands pried clams out of my
sticky mud amid sounds that could
only be understood as joyful.

The first people of the east had found me, and
with shouts of gratitude, drank, washed,
and delighted in me.

8

These Wampanoag people became part of my
landscape.   They came during the times of
sunlight like the deer and the ducks.

They pulled shiny bass and yellow perch
from me with lines and spears.

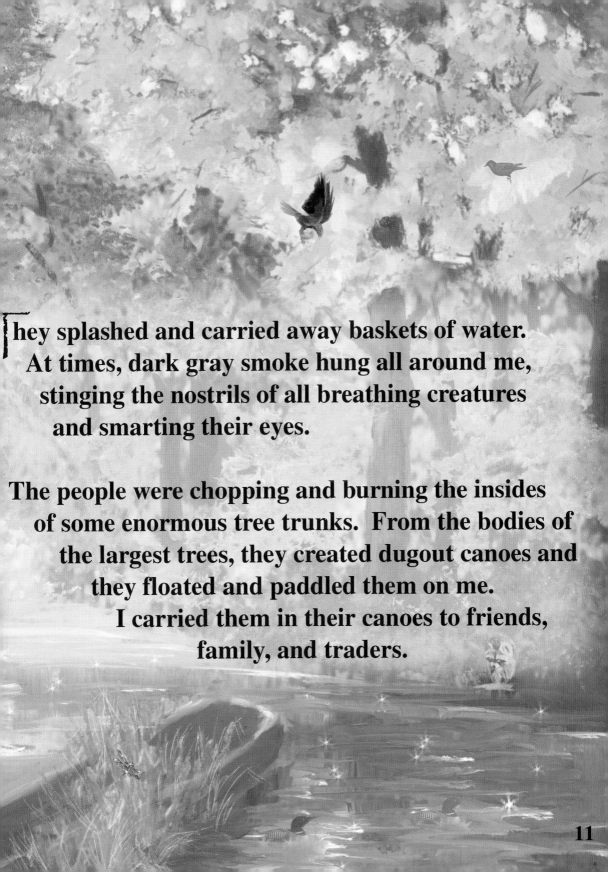

They splashed and carried away baskets of water.
At times, dark gray smoke hung all around me,
stinging the nostrils of all breathing creatures
and smarting their eyes.

The people were chopping and burning the insides
of some enormous tree trunks. From the bodies of
the largest trees, they created dugout canoes and
they floated and paddled them on me.
I carried them in their canoes to friends,
family, and traders.

11

At night, a dark velvet blanket with twinkling points of light crept over me. The people yielded quietly to prowling foxes, shuffling porcupines, gliding owls, and other marvelous nocturnal creatures.

Steadily, night gave way to sunlight, just as day gave way to darkness. Leaves grew gold and crimson, air turned crisp, snow fell and glistened like a million tiny diamonds, then softly melted away.

13

Shrubs and flowers grew, were washed by rains and baked by the hot sun. Every form of life imaginable teemed around me, was born, thrived, and died, as day chased night again and again, summer surrendered to winter over and over...

and yet again...

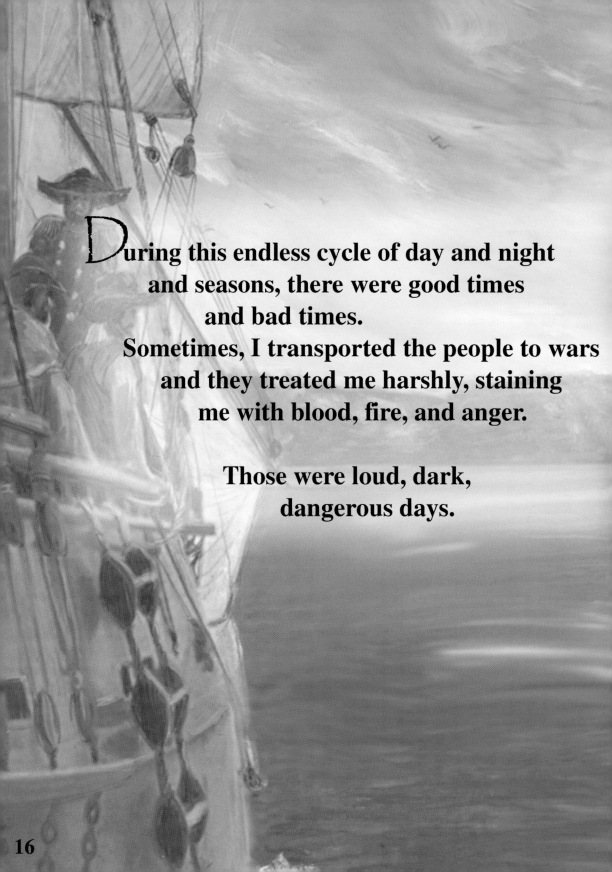

During this endless cycle of day and night
and seasons, there were good times
and bad times.
Sometimes, I transported the people to wars
and they treated me harshly, staining
me with blood, fire, and anger.

Those were loud, dark,
dangerous days.

After the unhappy days went away,
I recovered.

Peace settled in and I took care
of the people.

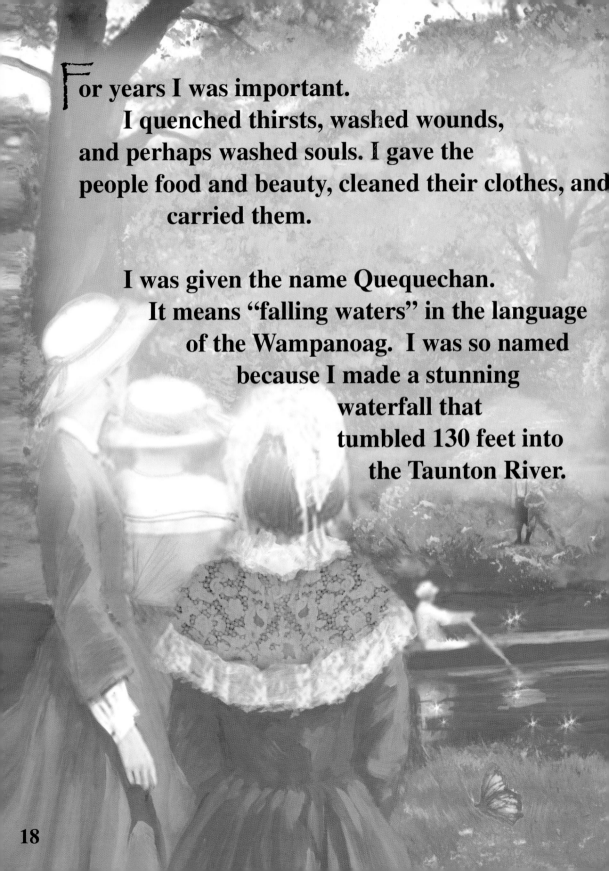

For years I was important.
I quenched thirsts, washed wounds,
and perhaps washed souls. I gave the
people food and beauty, cleaned their clothes, and
carried them.

I was given the name Quequechan.
It means "falling waters" in the language
of the Wampanoag. I was so named
because I made a stunning
waterfall that
tumbled 130 feet into
the Taunton River.

Reeds, grasses, trees, and vines drank nutrients
from my banks and grew lush and strong into
the whispering breeze.

The lily pads, nature's cups and saucers, wanted
me. Without my shiny table, they would have
no place to grow.

The dragonflies, quiet little airplanes, wanted me.
They lived their lives soaring over me
with amazing grace, doing their
dragonfly deeds.

The furry brown muskrats wanted me.
They drank, dived, and demanded little
else but this place to eat, sleep,
grow, and reproduce.

The sleek swimming mink wanted me.
They loved my shoreline buffet of
frogs, mice, and insects.

Painted turtles and snapping turtles wanted
to swim in my pool and sunbathe
on my rock patios.

I was wanted.

Years later...

The textile factories wanted me.

All around me rose huge mill buildings
   full of sweating workers.
People needed my muscles to turn their
   towering paddle wheels, so
I gave them my energy to run their machines.

They wanted me to remove their wastes, too.

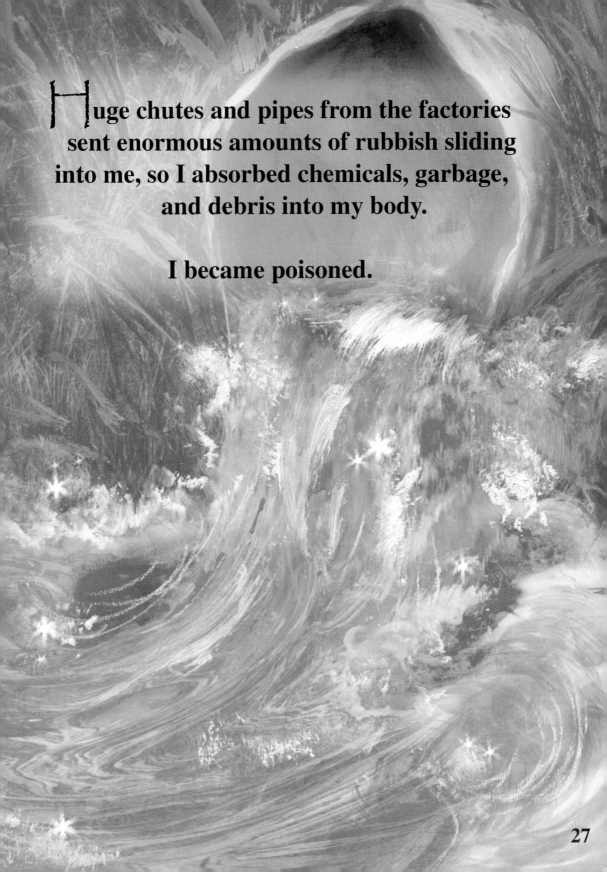

Huge chutes and pipes from the factories sent enormous amounts of rubbish sliding into me, so I absorbed chemicals, garbage, and debris into my body.

I became poisoned.

The civil authorities wanted me.
It was easier to build highways over
my openness than to wrench away
trees and blast through ledges.

Where I flowed in their way, they captured
me and my plants and animals in dark
pipes, blocking out the sun.

I traveled hidden,
under a speeding highway.

29

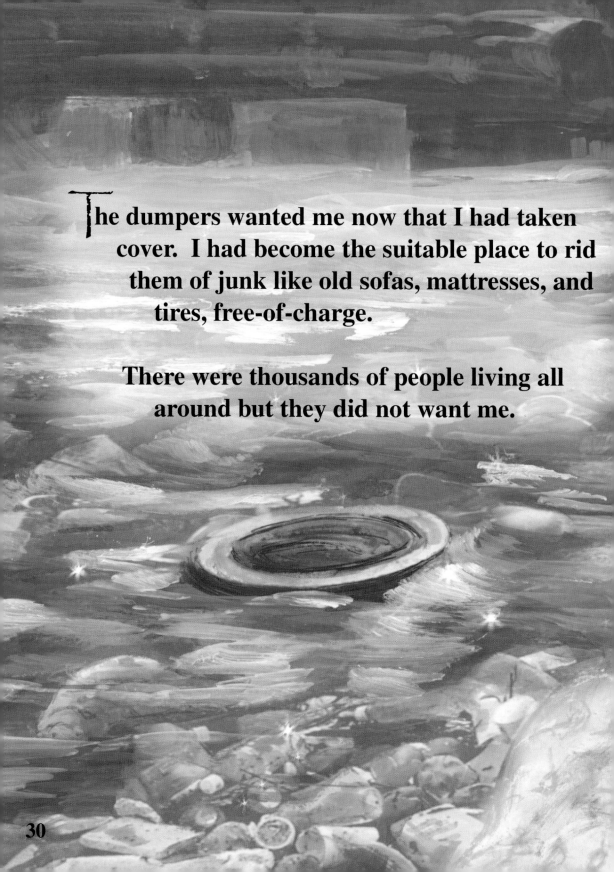

The dumpers wanted me now that I had taken cover. I had become the suitable place to rid them of junk like old sofas, mattresses, and tires, free-of-charge.

There were thousands of people living all around but they did not want me.

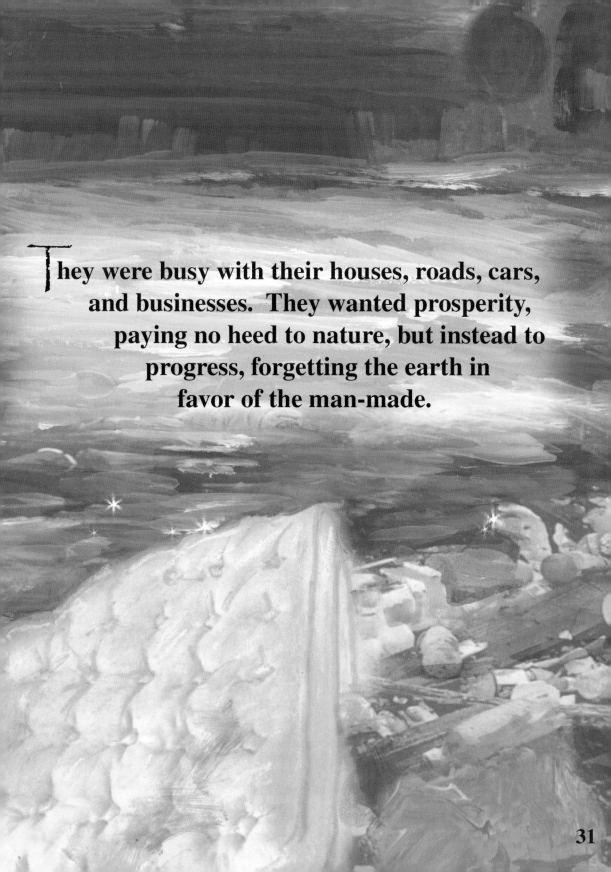

They were busy with their houses, roads, cars, and businesses. They wanted prosperity, paying no heed to nature, but instead to progress, forgetting the earth in favor of the man-made.

People covered the soil with pavement and
houses, and forgot about it. They hurried
by in air-conditioned cars with stout panes of glass
hemming them in, and shields of metal
blocking me out.
Little did the native
Wampanoag know, when naming me
"falling waters," that
I would fall into pieces,
later falling into oblivion.

33

Today, though the surface of my abandoned
waters shimmers in the sunlight as beautifully
as it did when the first inhabitants came,
very few people know what I look like.

Heedless of the trash below, my birds sing as
brightly and my plants flutter as greenly,
though very few people know I exist.

Despite man's attempt to muffle me, my scent
wafts sweetly across me in various flavors
from spring, summer, and autumn,
but no one notices.

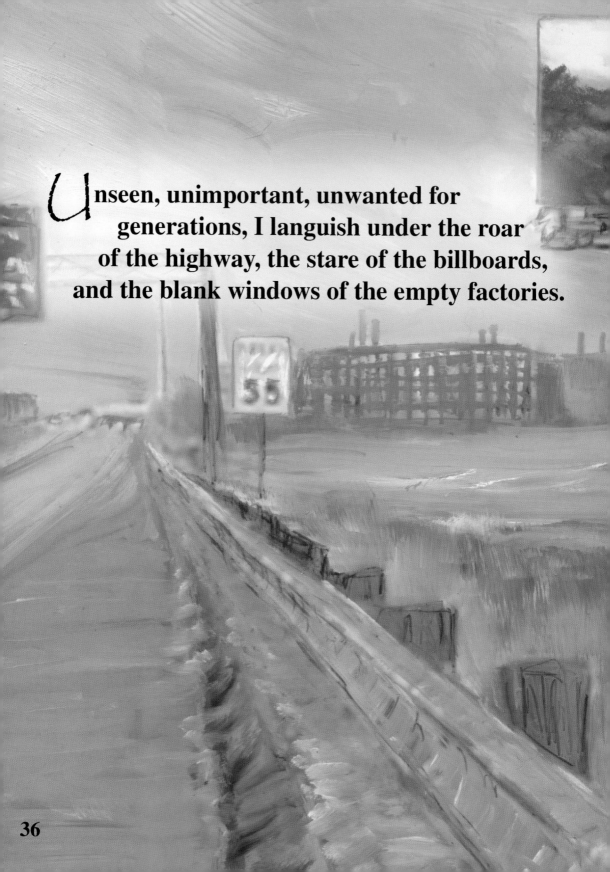

Unseen, unimportant, unwanted for
generations, I languish under the roar
of the highway, the stare of the billboards,
and the blank windows of the empty factories.

Help Save
our
River

I am a hidden, forgotten jewel
that shines unseen.

37

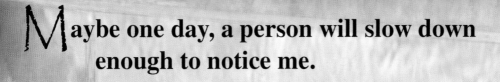

Maybe one day, a person will slow down
enough to notice me.

Maybe some nearby residents will realize that
they have a river. They might want to
rid me of refuse, waste, litter,
and loneliness.

WE
RECYCLE

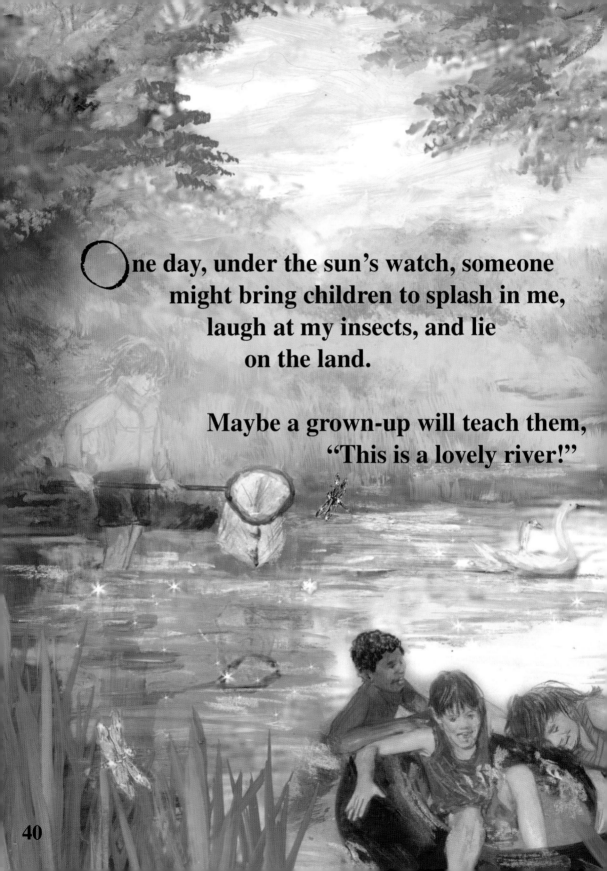

One day, under the sun's watch, someone
might bring children to splash in me,
laugh at my insects, and lie
on the land.

Maybe a grown-up will teach them,
"This is a lovely river!"

41

Maybe one day...
they'll want me,
the Quequechan River,
the falling waters.

The Wampanoag Language

These words are approximations of words from the Wampanoag language. Although efforts are being made to revive the language, it has not been used for at least a hundred years, so pronunciation is uncertain.

Page 6
Nippe!- Water!
Wawpatucke!- Canada Goose!
Hammos!- Fish!

Page 8
Wampanoag--The name means
"people of the dawn,"
or "people of the east."

Page 18
Quequechan means "falling waters."
Quequechan is pronounced quik-a-shan.

The Quequechan River is located in Fall River, Massachusetts.

About Operation Outreach-USA

Operation Outreach-USA (OO-USA) provides free literacy and character education programs to elementary schools across the country.

Because reading is the gateway to success, leveling the learning field for at-risk children is critical. By giving books to children to own, confidence is built and motivated readers are created. OO-USA selects books with messages that teach compassion, respect, and determination. OO-USA involves the school and the home with tools for teachers and parents to nurture and guide children as they learn and grow.

More than one million children in schools in all fifty states have participated in the program thanks to the support of a broad alliance of corporate, foundation, and individual sponsors.

To learn more about Operation Outreach-USA and how to help, visit www.oousa.org, call 1-800-243-7929, or email info@oousa.org.